Smart Shark

Written by Zoë Clarke

Illustrated by Lee Cosgrove

The best thing on Mark's worn and torn tablet was the Smart Shark map.

The map on the screen
had lots of sharks on it.

When a shark flashed on the map,
Mark ran to the right spot.

He had to zap the shark.

Morgan was in the park. She had Smart Shark on her tablet, too.

I wish I had ten shark crowns!

Morgan had tracked six sharks.

Mark spotted a shark!

He turned and darted right.

Morgan spotted the shark, too! She ran to the trees and bumped into Mark.

Morgan was too short to get one shark, so Mark got it for her.

Mark was too big to get one shark.

Morgan got the shark for him.

Morgan and Mark now had ten Smart Shark crowns!

The tablets went BEEP. They were at the top of the Smart Shark list!

Mark and Morgan started a Smart Shark club in the park.

They meet next to the arch and track crowds of sharks!

Talk about the story

Ask your child these questions:

1 What did Mark do when a shark flashed on his map?

2 How many sharks did Morgan have on her card at the start of the story?

3 Why did Mark need Morgan's help when he couldn't get to one of the sharks?

4 Do you think the Smart Shark club is popular? How can you tell?

5 Do you prefer playing games on a tablet or in real life?

6 What is your favourite game to play? Is it better when you play it with a friend?

Can your child retell the story in their own words?